Chang e what we are made of. The beauty is in the Possibilities!

It's Not Luck

Overcoming You.

by Michelle A. Mras
www.MichelleMras.com

Published by Vertex Learning, LLC

Denver, CO, Dayton-Cincinnati, OH, San Diego, CA Washington DC Atlanta, GA St. Louis, MO

Cover Photo: Barry (Ki) Quilloy, iTunes "K.I."
Cover Art: www.KerriGDesigns.com

ISBN-13: 978-1979299053

ISBN-10: 1979299056

Library of Congress Cataloging-in-Publication Data
Mras, Michelle, Author
Title: It's Not Luck-Overcoming You
Vertex Learning, LLC 2018

Contents

Also by Michelle Mras

Michelle's first book
Eat, Drink & Be Mary:
A Glimpse into a Life Well Lived
ISBN-13: 978-1495197635,
ISBN-10: 1495197638
Available at Amazon and Barnes & Noble
Paperback and Kindle

Message from the Author

Sometimes life has a funny way of redirecting you from the path you believe you should be on. Many of us hold jobs we never wanted but stay with them because we need to make a living - allowing us to do selfish activities like eating and having a place to sleep at night. We do what we think we need to, but there is an aching inside that something is missing.

When you see someone whom you consider successful, do you think, "They are so lucky! Look at the amazing life they lead?" Do you follow that thought with, "I could never do that," or some other downplay of your capabilities? Then, there is that voice in your head that often speaks at the most inopportune times, offering gems like, "You are a failure," "You aren't good enough," "Who do you think you are?" - You know the voice.

For most of my life, I was very up close and personal with the voice in my head. So much so, that I decided to write this book and share how I pushed through everything that the voice said – the voice that was keeping me stuck in a rut. You see, it's not luck. The answer revolves around calming the voice in your head – in essence, overcoming yourself. This book will have you ask yourself the same questions I asked myself. This book will teach you to overcome your greatest obstacle and critic – you! It is my sincerest wish that you will not only be successful, but also that you will be able to prosper regardless of the life challenges that you will face.

In May of 2014, I was in an auto accident that changed my life trajectory. I suffered a Traumatic Brain Injury (TBI) and had long and short-term memory loss. Years of my life, including knowledge gained through my college degrees, were virtually wiped out. My ability to handle crowds, loud noises and too much activity was gone. Doing any activity for more than 15 minutes would give me a massive migraine-like head pain from which it took weeks to recover.

There were several months in which I was only

cognizant for only about three hours in the morning; then I would lose my ability to form words or speak. I had to relearn my physical and mental limits and how to function with a memory that was not retaining or recalling events or people when needed. The voice in my head grew stronger and said I was useless (and it didn't matter if I could talk or not.)

The voice said I lost my memory because my life was not worth remembering. I cried myself through each miserable day, assaulted continually by the voice in my head. The days blended into months. I wanted my life to be a positive experience. I needed to thrive through my brain injury recovery without suffering from the internal voice that only belittled me. According to the voice, the only positive thing I had done in my life was marrying a good man; the only reason our children were remarkable was because I had married the right man.

If you're a movie buff, I was very much like Drew Barrymore's character in '50 First Dates'. Spoiler alert: In the movie, the main character's love interest has a brain injury that causes her to forget the previous day upon waking each morning. To those who didn't know me, I seemed perfectly fine. Those who were close to me knew the struggle that I had just forming simple thoughts and sentences. Those who were close to me and saw me daily, were aware of the months when I couldn't speak at all and how often I refused to leave home. I forgot words, dates, people, and names. I quite often forgot what I wanted or needed to do... or even worse, what I was doing. I forgot to eat. While driving, I often got lost, even on streets that were familiar to me.

I needed to find a solution to fight back against the voice. I needed a solution to get my life back.

I began journaling my days just to capture what was happening in my life and my head. Was I going insane? Every morning, I would read what I had written the day before to remind myself of what had happened. More importantly, I wanted to examine how often the voice was wrong. I even examined my journaling process, which led me to create this workbook. I'll get back to the workbook in a little bit - I promise!

My husband started writing me daily reminders. He programmed every location that I needed to go to into my car's navigation system. I worked hard to rebuild the neuro-pathways of my brain with traditional and non-traditional therapy. I never missed an appointment with the neurologist at the Warrior Recovery Center clinic at Ft Carson, Colorado and used Low Energy Neuro-Feedback System (LENS) through Harmonized Brain Centers in Colorado Springs. I got better, only to relapse. The doctors told me that it could take up to three years to get to "my new normal."

I slowly regained my ability to speak, although we had no idea if it was permanent or not. Every brain is different. To test my recovery, I auditioned for TEDx Colorado Springs, which is a locally organized Technology, Entertainment and Design (TED) Talks. TEDx is "a nonpartisan nonprofit devoted to spreading ideas, usually in the form of short, powerful talks." (www.TED.com) I considered it my "Go big or go home" approach to life before I possibly lost all of what made me...me. To my surprise, I made it into the lineup.

On October 17, 2015, I spoke to a live audience of several hundred people with my topic, *Eat, Drink and Be Mary: A Glimpse into a Life Well Lived*. It was a dedication to Mary - my mother-in-law's wisdom and strength through her life and battle with leukemia. I shared how the lessons learned from her helped me find the strength to battle through my TBI to help others live a full life. When I came off stage, I had no recollection of what I had said. It wasn't until I was able to watch the video did I realize what I had accomplished.

Soon after, I wrote my first book, which has the same name as the TEDx talk. It gave more background on my life with Mary, examples of her quirky wisdom, and why, even though she has passed, I still love her so much. If you want to know more, watch my talk at: www.MichelleMras.com or purchase the book.

I began to believe my life changing saga was almost over. Surviving and living with a TBI is no small feat. Memory loss didn't bother me because I had no idea what I had lost - I simply couldn't remember. I had calendar alerts appear on my phone reminding me of meetings. I decided to attend one and see if attending would help trigger memories. The first one I attended was a Toastmasters meeting. Everyone in the room knew me, but not one face looked familiar.

One man approached me after the meeting and acted as if we were longtime friends. I apologized to him that I had been in a car accident and I didn't recall who he was, but I sensed he was my friend. I told him my greatest fear was that my head was emptying and I would never return to be the real me again. He informed me that I was a wonderful speaker and leader in Toastmasters. He suggested, "Fill it back up!"

To solve my "problem," I joined the John Maxwell Team to regain and learn new skills to make up for all that I had lost. It was a slow process with the added challenge of my memory issues, but short-term does eventually move to long-term memory. Once again, my life had changed. I began to help others break through their fears and accomplish more than they believed possible. Through their growth, I grew. Slowly, more of my past memories came back to me. By journaling and pushing past my fears of what I may or may not be capable of achieving, I was lessening the verbal onslaught of attacks upon my confidence – the voice in my head was forced to quiet down.

I began 2016 feeling unstoppable. I published my first book, I had a few coaching clients, and I was back to 80% of the real me. In June, I began to feel something was wrong.

My brain began tingling again, and I became more forgetful. I felt as if I was regressing back to the early months of my brain injury. The voice in my head started its full campaign of how I "did too much," "pushed too hard," and "will lose everything for being stubborn." I eventually went in to see my doctor and asked for tests, scans and blood work.

On October 31st, a dermatologist told me that she believed I had a rare condition called Paget's disease of the breast - an outward manifestation of breast cancer. On November 16th, my surgeon told me the biopsy results were positive - I had breast cancer. The only way to stop this cancer was by getting a bi-lateral mastectomy. On December 19th, I had that surgery to save my life.

The voice in my head now had cancer as an additional, more potent weapon to use against me. This time, the voice said, "You're going to die a long painful death," "You aren't lucky enough to be a breast cancer survivor," "Do what you can before you die."

This was a terrifying time of my life.

I had started this book prior to the cancer diagnosis. This book was originally intended to be a light-hearted view of life. Cancer has changed that. Now, it's my chance to fashion a physical weapon to fight back against the negative voices inside my head. These are the questions I asked and continually ask myself when I doubt myself.

More importantly, this book is my opportunity to help you fight back against the voices in your head, to help you through your stories and your journeys regardless of the intensity.

My intention is to help you find correlating stories from your own life to help you reason with and conquer the negative voices in your head. When you read a chapter, think of what story from your own life comes to mind. Recalling your own stories will aid your mind to develop the answers to the questions that follow.

The questions at the end of each chapter are sometimes difficult to answer. Trust me, I understand how hard they are. Self-reflection is difficult when dealing with your own worst critic... yourself. You can do it! I believe that, once you get a glimpse of how fabulous you truly are, you will begin to question the voices that keep you from achieving whatever it is that you want to achieve.

> Believe in yourself
> and all that you are.
> Know that there is
> something inside
> of you that is
> greater than
> any obstacle.

Christian D. Larson

My dear friend, Dr. Paul R. Scheele, CEO of Scheele Learning Systems and Co-founder of Learning Strategies Corporation, once said, "If we were not created for change, we would be a world of crawlers." I had an epiphany! Pain is part of growth. Change is inevitable.

I encourage you, before you read much further,

to designate a notebook for the journey we will take together through this workbook. Write down a big crazy goal and write it in a positive tone.

Positive tone example: I want to be accurate and punctual with my work projects.

Negative tone example: I don't want to have errors or be late with my work projects.

In the beginning, the goal doesn't have to be Specific, Measurable, Achievable, Realistic & Time-related (S.M.A.R.T.). As we take this journey together, your goal will evolve to be S.M.A.R.T.

The questions at the end of each chapter are the same ones that I have used (and still use) to challenge the voice in my head through my biggest hurdles.

Use these questions and repeat the journey for every challenge you face, big or small.

Write out your goal and place it where you can't help but see it every day. Read your goal every morning. Read your goal every evening before you go to bed. Read your goal whenever the voice in your head speaks up.

In the notebook, write your goal as you start each chapter. When you finish the chapter, write out your answers to the chapter questions. Develop your own stories that relate to that chapter. Reflect on each experience to guide you through the question process. Finish the chapter by writing your goal again. Don't be alarmed if you want to modify your goal, adjust it when you feel the need to adjust it. Then, when you're ready, move on to the next chapter.

At the end of this workbook, you will have a better understanding of how much more potential you have. Continued use of the workbook will expose you to possibilities that you never knew existed.

You will come to realize that the voice inside your head is encouraging you to live a small life, to be less than the amazing person you are destined to be.

You may never be able to quiet the voice in your head (I still struggle with it), but you can certainly show the voice how wrong it is. I found through my life struggles that the voice inside my head is very strong. Once it stopped pushing and holding me back, I moved forward. When it walked by my side and even began encouraging me toward my life goals, I took leaps of faith the old me would never have dared.

Your inner voice will become your friend, too. Through the stories and questions this book provides, the negative voice will come to understand it can relax and trust you to move toward your goals.

---

*The real difficulty
is to overcome
how you think
about yourself.*

Maya Angelou

---

*If you think the cause of
your problem is "out there,"
you'll try to solve it from
the outside.*

*Take the shortcut:
Solve it from
within.*

Byron Katie

What to Expect:

- Maximize the positives; minimize the negatives.

- A voice can be positive or negative. The trick is to learn which is which.

- Know what is real versus what is perceived.

- Know that you can trust and depend upon yourself.

- Know that you can be happy and fulfilled.

- Know that you are important and have something to contribute to the world.

- Know that S.M.A.R.T. goals are attainable and you can overcome negative self-talk (the voice in your head).

- The voice is a guardian who wishes to keep you safe from all possible perceived danger. Anything it has not witnessed you accomplish is considered dangerous.

Once you realize these points, your potential is limitless!

Acknowledgments

My husband, Michael, who loves me more than I can even fathom, and I dearly love him for that and so much more.

My children, who put up with my endless desire to write throughout my medical hurdles. Their love and willingness to answer all my deep questions have helped me organize my thought processes.

My family and friends, who have supported me throughout my lifetime. There are too many to name; you know who you are. I've told you.

My In-Laws, Mary (R.I.P.) and Tony Mras who raised an amazing man and husband for me.

My business mentor, Joan Dixon (R.I.P.) for believing in my potential when I felt defeated.

Margaret and Chris Haché, my Canadian friends, who are the most amazing humans on this planet for having edited and re-edited my random thoughts into coherent English.

The John Maxwell Team, for being my JMT-DNA family. There are far too many of you to mention for having inspired me and for lifting me up while I was down.

Nancy and Bob Kittridge, for always being within reach when I was too scared to move forward. Bob was the friend who advised me to fill my brain with John Maxwell knowledge by joining the John Maxwell Team.

Harmonized Brain Centers, for not using the staple gun to hold down all those wires onto my scalp. LENS has helped me focus, release from pain, and move forward in my purpose.

Warrior Recovery Center, Ft. Carson, Colorado, for helping me get my balance back and my eyes to work together again. The mental and physical coordination work was tough, but you got me standing on my feet again. Thank you for serving the men and women who serve our country throughout their trials and rehabilitation.

Carol Myers, for her amazing listening skills

and especially her use of Eye Movement Desensitization and Reprocessing (EMDR). You guided me to realize that I could unlock and step through the door that I had perceived myself to be locked behind.

Scheele Learning Systems and Learning Strategies (Paul Scheele, PhD), for opening my mind to the possibilities that lay ahead. I will forever be a cheerleader for the work you do with the other than conscious mind. You are beautifully brilliant!

Cheryl Valk and the rest of the Ultimate You family, for holding me through my transitions and believing in me.

Barry (Ki) Quilloy for allowing me to use a photo of him for this book cover. Check out his music on iTunes, Six 'O Clock in Heaven by K.I. is one of my favorites.

Each of you holds a very special place in my heart.

Family and friends can be synonymous.
There are times when you encounter
life obstacles - when
you need a guide.
Reach out to others outside
your sphere of influence -
where
strangers become mentors,
mentors become friends,
and
friends become family.
Thank you to all
my family.

Michelle Mras

Chapter 1

Introduction

*Go confidently in
the direction of your
dreams!
Live the life
you've imagined.*

Henry David Thoreau

Somewhere around second grade, I learned the most shocking truth of my young life - I'm not just an American. I distinctly remember the teacher asking me what my heritage was and I said proudly, "American!" She replied, "You are made up of different races. American isn't a race. Ask your parents tonight when you get home."

Being the strong-willed child I was I marched home, determined to return to school the next day with the same answer. When my family gathered around the dinner table, I asked (more like told) my parents, "I'm an American, right? My teacher is wrong. She said I'm made up of races and American isn't a race." My parents looked at each other and then smiled at me, and my father answered, "Yes, we're American, but your mother is of Philippine descent, and I am of French Creole descent. Basically, you are half Filipino and half Black."

I felt tunnel vision hit me hard; the world began to spin. This couldn't be true! My young mind raced with so many thoughts, and I did everything to hold back the tears. I bit my bottom lip and calmly asked to be excused from the table. I ran down the hall to hide in the closet - somewhere I could be alone with my thoughts. As soon as I shut the door behind me, a flood of tears and uncontrolled sobbing rushed out of me. All I could think of was all the wonderful things I wanted to do when I grew up; and now, my dreams were gone.

It felt as though a lifetime had passed when there was a knock on the closet door. My mother slowly peeked her head in, "What's wrong?" Through my sobbing, I began to explain how my life was over:

"It doesn't matter how good I am at school; I can't be anything else but a slave or a house girl. I might be able to be a garbage man, but I'm too little." Both parents looked completely perplexed, so I continued. "In school, I read that black people are slaves. I saw them all chained up together and working in fields. Filipino girls become house girls. I don't want to be a slave!"

After a good muted chuckle, my parents pointed out that neither they, my immediate family nor anyone in my extended family were slaves in the last two generations. They also pointed out that house girls and garbage men help keep our houses clean and our communities clean, and that it isn't bad to be either. Then, they assured me that I'm not pre-destined to be anything because of either of my races.

Looking back at that naive moment in my life, I became acutely aware of how often we set limits on ourselves based off irrational data from our past:

- I can't do "X" because I didn't make the honor roll while in school.

- I'm not good enough for love because the love of my life in 6th grade broke my heart.

- That's not for me; other people deserve that life.

- It's not possible for me to pass/succeed/excel because....

You have not,
because you believe not.

John C. Maxwell

Action exercises

Write out the answers to the questions below. Even better, also discuss the questions and your answers with a loved one.

1. What would a dream life look like for you?

   _____

   _____

   _____

   _____

2. What would you go after if you knew you couldn't fail?

   _____

   _____

   _____

   _____

3. If you were to leave this world right now, would you be content with what you've done here and who you've become?

_____

_____

_____

_____

4. When it's all over and someone is summing up your life and the kind of person you are, what do you think they would say?

_____

_____

_____

_____

5. What do you think is keeping you from living your dream life?

_____

_____

_____

Dream big.
Build steps
toward it.
When you see
progress,
take leaps of faith.

Michelle Mras

Chapter 2

Are you stuck?

My youngest child, as a toddler, was an escape artist. If I didn't keep a sharp eye on her, she would find herself in all sorts of predicaments. One day, I was deeply engaged in the task of clearing out the closet while my two children played quietly behind me in the same room. When I turned around, there was a tea party of one. Where did the other little one go?

I checked the usual locations - the bathroom and my bedroom. No sign of my toddler. As I turned the corner into the living room, my eye caught a glimpse of movement about 12 feet up at the top of the staircase across the room. Lo and behold, on the outside of the staircase, holding onto the railing with all her might, was my toddler. She was gripping tightly and pulled in as close as possible to the railing with her tiny toes on the little bit of stair that protruded past the rails.

"Mikayla, mommy's here. Can you please come back down?"

I moved directly under her just in case she slipped.

She was obviously aware of how high she was as she whimpered out in desperation, "Mommy, help! I'm stuck!"

Initially, I wanted to run to the top of the staircase to save her, then decided against it. She made it up; she could make it down. Plus, I could catch her from below far easier than pulling her to safety from above.

"Don't look down," I said, "I'm right below you. Just work your way back to the bottom. Can you do that?"

I heard a faint, "Yes" as she nodded her little head and tentatively worked her way down one step at a time. I followed directly below her all the way. When she reached the bottom, she looked back to where she was stuck and exclaimed, "Wow! I was way up high!" She was amazed at how high she had gone and proud of herself for making it back down.

How often do we find ourselves stuck without fully understanding how we got where we did?

My daughter had accomplished a huge task but became stuck once she realized how far she had gone. How often do we get stuck at the pinnacle of accomplishing something great?

Everything
you want
is on
the other side
of
fear.

Jack Canfield

Action exercises

Write out the answers to the questions below. Even better, also discuss the questions and your answers with a loved one.

1. Where are you stuck in your life?

   _____

   _____

   _____

   _____

2. What's holding you back? Fear? Something else?

   _____

   _____

   _____

   _____

3. When was the last time you did something you've never done before?

   _____

_____

_____

_____

4. In vivid detail, imagine yourself being past your "sticking point." What does your life look like? What does it sound like? What does it feel like? Now, what steps do you need to take to get yourself past your sticking point?

_____

_____

_____

_____

5. Or, if the last question in #4 doesn't work for you, how about, "If you fall, who are the people that would be there to catch you?"

_____

_____

_____

_____

Take risks:
If you win,
you will be happy.
If you lose,
you will be wise.

Unknown

Chapter 3

Who Is Going to Do It for You?

In my early forties, I went to Oahu, Hawaii to visit two of my Ohana (extended family) brothers, Ki and Pono. My mother and younger sister went with me on the trip. On our first day at the beach, we were walking along the water's edge toward a concrete embankment. The two men were helping my mother on the slick wall ledge, my sister was far ahead, and I was trailing well behind them picking up shells along the way. I had Ki's very expensive camera in my left hand. I would occasionally snap a photo of the water, a peculiar shell, or my family ahead of me. I heard Pono yell back to me, "Watch the third wave! It's strong!"

I ignored the warning since I was only in

three inches of water, and just at the edge of the wave. I continued to walk slowly, but had now turned my back to the ocean to pick up several beautiful shells. I heard yet another warning, "Never turn your back to the ocean!" Once again, I ignored him. The tide was coming in, but it was still low to me. I bent down again, when SWOOSH! The third wave hit the back of my knees and knocked me face down into the water. I felt my cheek hit a large slimy rock and the tide started to pull me toward the ocean.

I struggled to stand up, but the undertow had a hold of me. The powerful tide pulled me further away from the beach until the next wave pushed me back. For no reason, I began to laugh uncontrollably while simultaneously struggling to stand back up. Remember Ki's camera I was holding? I did. Each time I went under, I raised my hand above (what I thought was) the water level. Each time the current pushed me into shallow water, everyone heard me laughing. Then, my head would go under as I was pulled out into the ocean. This happened multiple times as my family watched confused on whether I was in trouble or enjoying myself.

I had lost the concept of imminent danger. Instead of helping myself with both hands, I continually tried to save the camera. I didn't see the need for me to save myself! Somewhere during my ordeal, Pono came back to check if I was laughing or drowning. During one of my submersions, I felt a large hand grasp my wrist and lift me out of the water like a fish at the end of a fishing line. He placed me upright back onto the beach and complained aloud, "Why are you laughing? You're drowning! How are you drowning in water not deep enough for my ankle?" Still laughing, I responded, "I was drowning. I couldn't get up, but I saved the camera." He mumbled something in Hawaiian, which probably involved words like, "crazy big island woman drowning in three inches of water."

Looking back at that experience, I realized

I was under the misconception that no harm would happen to me. I'm in paradise with my Ohana, and I had a higher respect for the expensive camera than on my own life. How often do we misinterpret a situation and place value on other things, people, a job, a status, etc. before our happiness and well-being?

How often do we not notice the warnings, or even ignore them? Something was pushing those shells far up on the beach, but I didn't acknowledge the force behind the movement. Not knowing the danger we are in precludes us from asking for help. Additionally, our outward appearance of confidence will prevent others from seeing our distress.

Your life, your happiness, must come from you. Once you are happy with who you are, and believe in you, the rest will easily follow suit.

- Know the difference between what is important and what is critical.
- You should not consider invested

money/costs on your path to fulfill-
ment. Once you realize that you are on
the wrong path for you, change direc-
tion and make a new path – even if
you have already paid for it. For exam-
ple, I didn't save myself from drown-
ing because I was so invested in the
price of the camera. I was drowning
trying to save the investment.

---

*Happiness
radiates like the
fragrance
from a flower
and draws
all good things
toward you.*

Maharishi Mahesh Yogi

Action exercises

Write out the answers to the questions below. Even better, also discuss the questions and your answers with a loved one.

1. Who do you depend on in your life?

   _____

   _____

   _____

   _____

2. For what do you depend on them?

   _____

   _____

   _____

   _____

3. Are there important things in your life that you are waiting for other people to deliver?

   _____

_____

_____

_____

4. What would it take for you to do what you are waiting for them to do?

_____

_____

_____

_____

5. What are you holding onto that is holding you from your path? Are you holding onto it because it carries a monetary value?

_____

_____

_____

_____

---

*Now I see that the
journey was never
meant to lead to some
new and improved
version of me;
that it has always been
about coming home
to who I already am.*

Katrina Kenison

Chapter 4

What do you really want?

When we were children, my older siblings and I would gather around the Christmas editions of the Sears and J.C. Penney catalogs. With a marker, we would circle all the awesome toys we wanted for Christmas. Did you ever do that? Nowadays, we are more likely to get a list of websites with everything our kids desire to be under the tree or in a box for their birthdays. Either way, isn't dreaming fun? My siblings and I would talk about all the great adventures and experiences we'd have if we only got (insert large outrageous gift here). Every year, we were thrilled to receive one of the randomly selected items on Christmas morning exclaiming, "Santa knew what I really wanted the most!" We had circled pretty much everything in the catalogs, so how could good old Santa miss?

In high school, I was asked to create a list of all the careers in which I might be interested. This request was in preparation for the ASVAB testing, which is an acronym for the Armed Services Vocational Aptitude Battery test. I'm not sure other high school students were required to take this test, but those of us at a Department of Defense (DOD) school, in my case, Wagner High School at Clark Air Base, Philippines did. This experience was the first time where I realized there were other jobs in the world that didn't revolve around military life. This challenged my previous answers for, "What do you want to be when you grow up?" After the test, my friends and I discussed how we thought we scored. Did we show aptitude for what we listed? When the scores finally came back, it was exciting to see all the possibilities for our future!

My next opportunity to make a list of my personal choices was in my first year of college. I had to create a list of the classes I

wished to take to fulfill the degree require-
ments of my chosen field of Industrial Engi-
neering. This list wasn't nearly as exciting as
the prior lists because there were fewer op-
tions. I found pleasure in deciding electives
outside of my field of concentration, since this
selection was far broader.

Each of these lists gave me pause to think
of what could be. As I've grown older, I've re-
alized what I wanted most wasn't offered in a
course. To be content, fulfilled, happy, and
loved would come from accomplishing some-
thing far deeper inside me as I sought and
crossed off the list of goals and desires of my
heart.

Lists are a handy tool to use when making
decisions, remembering what is important to
us, remembering what needs to be done, and
simply as a good memory aid. Just be sure
that the list for what you want in life includes
words like content, fulfilled, happy, and loved.

No one departs this life regretting not
completing that last report on their checklist.

They regret not living life as they wished they could have; being too scared to be daring; not spending more time with their family and friends; being too serious; or not pursuing their dream goals.

Desire:
The starting point
of all achievement.

Napoleon Hill

Action exercises

Write out the answers to the questions below. Even better, also discuss the questions and your answers with a loved one.

1. When was the last time you sat down and listed all the things you want?

   _____

   _____

   _____

   _____

2. In which areas of your life are you really content with?

   _____

   _____

   _____

   _____

3. In which areas of your life are you not
   content with?

   _____

   _____

   _____

   _____

4. Did you edit your list since you initially
   wrote it?

   _____

   _____

   _____

   _____

5. If you did edit your list, why?

   _____

   _____

   _____

   _____

6. If you didn't edit your list, why not?

_____

_____

_____

_____

_____

Hope and fear
cannot occupy
the same space
at the same time.
Invite one
to stay.

_____

Maya Angelou

Chapter 5

What is real, the danger or the fear?

D o you remember the carefree nursery song about the Itsy Bitsy Spider? As a child, I loved singing it, until the summer of '76. My brothers, three of our young uncles and I were racing bikes through the open halls of the elementary school at Clark Air Base, Philippines. Being the youngest, I was riding on the back of the banana seat with my Uncle Will. We were riding so fast and I was screaming, "Warp factor 2, Sulu!" while having the time of my life.

I don't know why I noticed but, suddenly, there was a spider web directly in our path. Normally, I wouldn't care but, this one was different - it was HUGE. It spanned the width of the hall, thick, white, and we were on a collision course with it at warp factor 2. I screamed, "Uncle Will watch out for the web! Watch out for the web!"

Have you ever had one of those moments when time slows so much that you can see everything in great detail and have no control of how to avoid it? This phenomenon happened to me at about three feet from the web. It wasn't the web that bothered me; rather, it was what was centered on the web.

There was a large spider about five inches long and two inches wide directly in the path of my face. It was big and black, with yellow markings. For those of you who said, "Eww" for the size ... that was just its body. Each of it's legs were an additional six inches long!

"Watch out for the...." I fell off the bike. I was no longer holding the waist of my uncle because I was gripping my neck and not breathing. You see, there was a battle going on. The spider was at the back of my mouth. Its body was between my tonsils and its legs were gripping the insides of my cheeks. I had locked my throat to stop it from going down. I couldn't breathe out of fear that any movement would force it down. My brother, Troy, ran over and began to help me as I was making the universal sign of choking.

Whop! Whop! Whop! Troy hit my back repeatedly to dislodge what was choking me.

GASP His attempts had the opposite effect of my desired outcome. The spider went down.

I was a tough little girl, but this was far too much for me to bear. I began bawling uncontrollably.

"Did you swallow a bug?" Nod.

"Was it the spider?" Nod.

"Was it big?" Nod.

"Don't worry. The spider probably wasn't that big. It was probably carrying an egg sack."

SOB

At that moment, the Itsy Bitsy Spider

nursery song was forever changed. Troy told me that I didn't hurt the baby spiders. He assured me that the babies would eventually work their way out of me. I instantly developed arachnophobia. Until my mid-teen years, I believed that the ancestors of the eaten banana spider would find me and take revenge. Yes, I understand that is irrational, but I believed it!

This fear crippled my ability to enjoy being outside while living on a tropical island. I avoided every location that I suspected could possibly hide an attacking spider. I feared the unknown. It took learning about biology to fully understand the effects of stomach acid on a spider and how the spider couldn't be alive crying out with its spider telepathy for help. Not until I knew this fact did I relinquished fear.

There are situations in my adult life where I have to remind myself of this experience. To put the current situation into perspective, I ask myself, "Is this a real fear?"

- Fears are acquired.

- Some fears are real; many are not.

- Many fears no longer make sense or no longer apply, but we hold onto them all the same.

We don't fear
the unknown.
We fear what
we believe
we know about
the unknown.

Robin Sharma

Action exercises

Write out the answers to the questions below. Even better, also discuss the questions and your answers with a loved one.

1. What causes you the most fear?

    _____

    _____

    _____

    _____

2. What are four other things that cause you to be afraid?

    _____

    _____

    _____

    _____

3. Are any of these five fears holding you back from what you want to achieve?

    _____

---

4. What would change in your life if you
   could overcome one or more of these
   fears?

---

5. What one small step can you take to move
   away from these fears?

_____

*By recording your
dreams
and goals on paper,
you set in motion
the process of
becoming the person
you most want to be.
Put your future in good
hands —
your own.*

_____

Mark Victor Hansen

Goal Check

Now is a good time to recheck your goal from when we started this journey. Believe it or not, goals change and the change is a positive sign that you are becoming "unstuck".

1. Has your original goal evolved? If so, how?

   _____

   _____

   _____

   _____

2. Is it a S.M.A.R.T. goal (Specific, Measurable, Achievable, Relevant and Time Related)? If not, now is a good time to make it S.M.A.R.T. Keep your language positive and present tense. Avoid the negative (i.e. I don't want to be...) Write for what you want, not what you don't want. How will you know if you achieved the goal? How is

it measured?

_____

_____

_____

_____

It can be as simple as, "My body feels/works better when it is 10 pounds lighter" or "I enjoy one cup of plain coffee per day". What action will you take to make the goal happen? For example, "I will move my body and raise my heart rate to 140 beats per minute for 30 minutes twice a week".

These examples are from my personal experience. When I realized I had cancer, I knew I needed to get my health under control to aid my body and prepare to battle this disease. I set a goal to release 10 pounds a month through eating healthier, watching my food portion size, eliminating sugar from my morning coffee, and walking every day. These small changes to my lifestyle added up to enormous successes. I released over 80 pounds in 8 months. Keep your goal statement reasonable. No one goes from the couch to marathon-ready in a week. Give yourself a time limit to accomplish the goal, but not an outrageous amount of time.

3. If your goal has changed, write it down, take down all instances of the old goal and replace it with your new goal. Additionally, write the new goal prominently in your notebook.

_____

_____

_____

_____

*You have to set goals
that are
almost out of reach.
If you set a goal that is
attainable without
much work or thought,
you are stuck with
something below your
true talent and
potential.*

Steve Garvey

Chapter 6

Who limits your potential?

In my first year of college, my major field of study was Industrial Engineering. My first assessment with my Academic Advisor is a day etched into my memory. The man who understood my engineering path shook my hand as I entered his office. He asked me how I was enjoying my coursework and eventually asked what I did in my free time. I responded that I really didn't have free time because I held four part-time jobs, along with my church duties. He informed me that I couldn't work and be an engineering student.

I responded, "Sir, I'm on my own. I have a scholarship, but I have to pay for my own housing, my car, insurance and food."

He became obviously irritated, raised his voice as he declared, "You might as well drop out now and save yourself the effort of obtaining an engineering degree!" He went on about how there were very few women in engineering. If I didn't have time to dedicate myself fully to the curriculum, I would never survive the work expected of me.

He ignored my attempts to explain that I had my work and school schedule perfectly balanced; he was obviously done speaking with me. I left that session sure that he was right, and my failure was imminent.

Quitting any of my jobs was out of the question. To get to my full schedule of classes, I had to break my work up in a way that a regular job would not allow. My only choice was to simply not fail. I would keep my GPA (grade point average) high enough to keep my scholarship. Each semester, when I entered his office for the assessment, he always appeared shocked that I was still in the program and maintaining my GPA. Although he didn't say the words again, the echo of what he said when we first met joined the chorus of voices

I already housed internally, "You will fail."

At the beginning of my 4th year, the voice became overwhelmingly powerful. Life was getting too complicated juggling jobs, school, and my faith all at once. I never considered that I had already been doing it, and doing it well, for the past three years. My GPA slipped and I lost my scholarship. I imagined the guidance counselor saying, "I knew it," "I was right," "Women don't belong."

There was no recovering. I couldn't work more to pay for school, so I dropped out.

The voice inside my head had won.

I no longer worked to pay for school to create a better career and a better life for myself. I now worked to survive. Without school, I did not have to work odd hours. I got a "real job." When my friend's mother learned that I needed a full-time job, she offered me a position as her administrative assistant at the Omaha Federal Credit Union.

Joan Dixon, who I affectionately referred

to as "Ms. D," took me under her wing. As her assistant, Ms. D would hand me a task; I would learn how to do it and create a process for it. She was a powerhouse of a woman who trusted me to do my best. I did my best to avoid disappointing her. Ms. D was my business mentor. I learned so much from her thrusting me into situations that were completely out of my comfort zone. On the rare occasion when I gave her a puzzled look about a new task, she would simply say, "You'll figure it out." Amazingly enough, I always did. She will always hold a special place in my heart. She is who I envision when I think of myself in the business world.

Unfortunately, even with all the positivity and support I received from Ms. D, the voice inside my head kept saying, "You're nothing without a degree." As years passed, I received my Associate of Arts degree, a Bachelor degree in Marketing Management and a Master degree of Quality Systems Management. I still felt I needed more. My husband called me

"The Scarecrow" from the Wizard of Oz, because I did not feel like I had a brain without a piece of paper to prove it. I had to look at the people I admire and consider to be wise to realize that many of the people whom I hold in high regard do not have college degrees.

*All our dreams
can come true,
if we have
the courage
to pursue them.*

Walt Disney

Action exercises

Write out the answers to the questions below. Even better, also discuss the questions and your answers with a loved one.

1. What is the biggest obstacle holding you back from taking the next step toward your goal or dream?

_____

_____

_____

_____

2. What other options can you identify rather than not moving forward?

_____

_____

_____

_____

3. Write out five different actions that you could take right now. They can be small actions. Movement forward toward your dream is better than no movement at all.

_____

_____

_____

_____

4. For the above actions, do you believe any will not work? If so, I want you to RE-ALLY think whether that's true, or if it could simply be the voice limiting your potential?

_____

_____

_____

_____

5. Is there anyone you know and admire who could deal with this differently? If so, what would they do?

_____

_____

_____

_____

_____

*How far you
can go in life
is yet to be seen.
Don't let other people's
limited beliefs
about what's possible
diminish your potential.*

_____

Kevin Ngo

Chapter 7

Sometimes the obvious isn't obvious.

During my early 20s, my husband and I lived in Tacoma, Washington. On one particular day, I was hanging out with my husband's former housemate, Paul. It was a beautiful, sunny day devoid of the rain clouds that normally threatened perfect days in the Pacific Northwest. There was a cool breeze coming off Puget Sound and we had the car windows opened with the wind blowing through our hair. We decided to go to a mall in downtown Seattle. We were having a good time laughing and listening to music on the radio. Normally, if we went somewhere together, either Michael or Paul would drive. Today, I was at the wheel.

We zoomed in my little car up the highway into Seattle without incident. We reached the mall area and were having difficulties finding parking. I do not like city traffic and get very nervous, especially faced with the prospect of parallel parking on a city street.

"Let's just find a garage," I stated. Then, I began nervously talking about where we could eat lunch. I always talk more when I'm nervous.

"Just loop around the block, someone's bound to leave." Paul suggested with a wave of his finger.

As I drove to go around the block, I started telling him the story about the time Michael and I went to the Space Needle for dinner.

"Paul, have you ever eaten there?" I didn't pause for an answer. "It is an exquisite place to eat with candlelit tables and fancy food. It was so neat to watch the skyline of Seattle through the windows of a revolving restaurant. I ordered a small carafe of wine and the salmon. Michael ordered the Prime Rib. When the food came, I took a bite of my rice pilaf and exclaimed, This rice pilaf is incredible! You should try it. Michael took a huge fork full off his plate and stuck it into his mouth. Immediately, his face turned red and he began to drink all the water and then my carafe of wine. He had accidentally eaten a fork full of freshly grated horseradish! The poor man planned to propose that night but he felt the mood was ruined by...."

"One way." Paul interrupted.

"Yeah, I guess, there is only one way to have Prime Rib, but...."

"One way." Paul calmly replied, again.

"Paul, what in the world are you talking about?" I said, a little confused and agitated that my story didn't amuse him.

"One-way street, Michelle" he replied in the calmest, nonchalant tone as if he was simply asking for lemon with his water.

In my mind, I was still confused. I kept looking at Paul as I glanced toward the front of the car. He was making no sense at all! I was talking about horseradish, and he's talking about one-way streets... reality dawned on me, "ONE-WAY STREET!" I screamed out.

That's why no other car had turned left with me as I went around the block. Paul had managed to warn me of our imminent danger as the light for on-coming traffic had turned green. We were in the middle lane as angry drivers honked their horns and swirled past us. Not once did Paul raise his voice or seem agitated at all. I was frozen, white-knuckled holding onto the steering wheel, my foot on the brake, and trying not to cry.

In an even tone, he simply said, "The cars have passed; now is a good time to move over to the side and make a U-turn to join the traffic flow. Move now." My grip made it difficult to steer, but I managed to follow his instructions. When we reached the side to make my U-turn, I pleaded for him to take the wheel. He told me there wasn't time, and that I could manage it. Paul was right. I turned the car around. I was so relieved; I began talking about how I almost killed us!

"Paul, how did you stay so calm? I would

have shown some emotion. Good grief! You will forever have the title 'The Man with Nerves of Steel!' You are the calmest person I've ever known...."

"Red," he replied.

"I know! You read the situation so well. You are simply "The Man."

"Red light, Michelle," he replied.

In my relief from one tight spot, I had inadvertently placed us into another by not stopping at the red light. Once again, cars managed to avoid hitting us. Paul simply smiled and shook his head.

How often have we tried to distract ourselves from what we fear? I was trying to talk over the voice in my head; I missed the clear, logical voice coming from a physical person sitting next to me. In times of high stress, it is helpful to have an outside perspective to help you see the bigger picture. Finding a person to guide you out of your rut can help keep you focused on where you plan to go.

Your way.
The other person's way.
God's way.
You can only control
one.

Paul R. Scheele, PhD

paraphrasing Byron Katie

I can find only three
kinds of business
in the Universe:
Mine,
Yours,
and God's.

Action exercises

Write out the answers to the questions below. Even better, also discuss the questions and your answers with a loved one.

1. Do you know anyone who is stuck in a key area of their life and yet has significant advantages from being stuck?

_____

_____

_____

_____

2. Where are you stuck in life?

_____

_____

_____

_____

3. What would someone who knows you well say is the reason you are not moving on?

_____

_____

_____

_____

4. There are coaches and mentors available to help you see the bigger picture of your life situations. Do you have someone to whom you can reach out? Who are they?

_____

_____

_____

_____

---

*Faith is taking
the first step
even when
you don't see
the whole staircase.*

Martin Luther King, Jr.

Chapter 8

You are perfect just as you are!

When I first met my husband, we were teenagers in high school. We would sit and talk for hours. Every few minutes he would comment, "You know, I'm right here. No need to project your voice." Project? I had no idea I was speaking loudly. What we discovered was my idea of a whisper was other people's normal speaking volume. I didn't know how to whisper. Perhaps it was my upbringing and being the fourth of six children. I had to speak up to be heard.

My brother used to tease me with a joke about a large-mouthed frog.

> *There once was a little frog with a very large mouth. He approached his mother one day and blasted her with his loud*

85

voice,

"Mama! Mama! What do alligators eat?"

"I don't know, perhaps you should ask Mr. Owl. He is wise." replied his mother.

So the little frog with the very large mouth went to Mr. Owl's tree and found Mr. Owl enjoying the beautiful song of the wind blowing through the trees. Mr. Owl was abruptly ripped from his serenity with the boisterous voice of the little frog.

"Mr. Owl! Mr. Owl! What do alligators eat?" inquired the little frog with a very large mouth.

Obviously irritated, Mr. Owl replied, "I don't know! Go ask Mr. Alligator. You can find him at the water's edge."

Off went the little frog with a very large mouth to find Mr. Alligator. When he reached the water's edge he saw Mr. Alligator sunning himself on a large rock.

He was so excited to find Mr. Alligator and get his answer that he spoke out louder so he could be sure Mr. Alligator could hear him,

"Mr. Alligator! Mr. Alligator! What do alligators eat?"

Mr. Alligator opened one eye and replied,

*"Frogs with big
mouths."*

*"Oh, really?" the little
frog with a very large
mouth softly responded
with his mouth as small
as possible.*

The joke always amused me. Honestly, until I began to write this chapter, I hadn't realized that my brother was trying to teach me about my issue. Suddenly, it's even more amusing. Anyway, after my discussion with my future husband about my volume, I concentrated on learning to control my voice. I constantly matched the volume of those around me. Then, one magical day, about 10-years later, my new husband looked at me with a smile and said, "You whisper very well! Did you realize you can officially whisper?"

This accomplishment took a lot of effort and to this day I remain diligent with modulating my voice for different situations. I used to worry about how others saw me. I never wanted to be the center of attention. Now, my ability to control my voice and project has become my biggest asset. What once embarrassed me is now my strength.

It's difficult and almost impossible to love others if you don't love yourself. Accept and embrace yourself as the unique individual you are. The attribute/scar/painful life experience we are most ashamed of is what makes us different and is the gift we should value the most and share with others.

Try to look at your weakness
and convert it
into your strength.
That's success.

Zig Ziglar

---

*Sometimes you don't
realize
your own strength
until you come
face to face
with your
greatest weakness.*

Susan Gale

Action exercises

Write out the answers to the questions below. Even better, also discuss the questions and your answers with a loved one.

1. What aspects of you are you not happy with?

   _____

   _____

   _____

   _____

2. How do these aspects affect your life?

   _____

   _____

   _____

   _____

3. Do you know anyone who has similar aspects and who are not bothered by the aspect at all, or even uses their aspect as an advantage?

_____

_____

_____

_____

4. How could it be true that your weaknesses are also your sensitivities?

_____

_____

_____

_____

5. Can you see that what you are most sensitive about, can actually be your strength?

_____

_____

_____

_____

_____

Every human has four
endowments -
self-awareness,
conscience,
independent will
and
creative imagination.
These give us the ulti-
mate
human freedom...
The power to choose,
to respond,
to change.

_____

Stephen Covey

Chapter 9

Love all life, including yourself!

Some of my experiences with family, school, relationships, and jobs left me very insecure. All the voices ganged up on me. The disappointment that I felt toward myself haunted many of my decisions.

A simple task such as ordering ice cream - I would stare into the case of the multiple flavors and simply ask for vanilla with chocolate chips. Did I order that because that's what I wanted? No. I ordered it because it was simple and I didn't want to waste everyone's time.

When I married my high school sweetheart, ten years after meeting him, I had to reevaluate the voice in my head that said I wasn't worthy of love. I married my soul mate. I married him because he believed in us. I trusted his opinion. Now, happiness surrounds me. The voice was wrong. How many other circumstances are there where the voice can be wrong?

I honestly did not want children, but my husband did. I was afraid that I would project my insecurities onto our children. In the end, I trusted my husband. When I became a mother, there were doubts about whether I could carry out the task of raising a small human. The voice in my head told me that if I couldn't survive on my own and finish college, how was I capable of bringing a child into the world and keep that child nourished and thriving? And yet, I have successfully raised my children! Again, the voice was wrong.

Children grow up. Once my babies were mobile and going to school, I became petrified with fear. I couldn't be with them to constantly protect them from the world, but I tried. When my children begged to ride their bikes to school, I would follow them with my car at a safe distance, making sure that they would be okay.

I hope my children truly forgive me for being ever-present in their lives. My voice told me countless terrifying stories of what could happen to unattended children. Once again, the voice was wrong. My children would not get lost on the sidewalk home while riding with eight of their best friends. A mountain lion wouldn't spontaneously roam the neighborhood to eat my children.

Our children are now young adults in college. They survived my imagination. I still worry, but our children have given me every reason to trust their decisions. Again, the voice was wrong.

My husband always says that college is about more than an education. All your life, you've been taught the morals of your parents. A college is a safe place where you are allowed to make mistakes. For our children, we set positive expectations, provide them with resources and the knowledge that we are here to support them when they need us, and set them free.

There is a song by Pink Floyd called, "Mother" that comes to mind. I didn't want to be Mama:

> *Mama's gonna make all your nightmares come true*
>
> *Mama's gonna put all her fears into you*
>
> *Mama's gonna keep you right here under her wing*
>
> *She won't let you fly but she might let you sing*
>
> *Mama's gonna keep baby cozy and warm*
>
> *Ooh, babe, ooh, babe, ooh, babe*
>
> *Of course Mama's gonna help build the wall*

I have discovered that the voice in my head that I thought was smarter than me, wasn't smarter than me after all.

The voice was much more often wrong than right.

I began testing the intelligence of the voice in my head. Whenever I was asked to try something the voice thought I'd be horrible at, I would push through my apprehension and do it anyway. Guess what? I was pretty decent at everything I tried!

Want to be a Quality Examiner? — Of course!

Want to be a Benefit Auctioneer? — Sure!

Have you ever thought of Public Speaking? — I'd love to try!

The list of jobs I've held is lengthy. When people ask what I've done, I say, "I've been a cook, a baker, a candlestick maker and all of the above."

Why?

Because I will try practically anything once and do it again, just to ensure that I have learned from the first time. This method applies to pretty much everything, except jumping out of a perfectly good plane. I have no desire to test if I'm good at that one at all. My friend and calmest driving parter ever, Paul has a shirt that has, "Initial success or absolute failure - Explosive Ordinance Disposal, EOD" printed on it. No thanks, I won't try disarming bombs either.

The magic of a new experience includes the people you meet and learn from, as well as the new skills acquired. My life, through the good and the not so good times, has been one learning event after another. Simply told, I enjoy learning and I thrive on education in whatever form. The biggest learning transformations that I have experienced have come through simply living life, giving back to my community and loving those around me.

None of my experiences would have been quite as fulfilling if I didn't forgive myself for the initially perceived major failures in my life. I had to accept that the inner voice telling me that I "wasn't good enough" was not all-knowing. I had to learn to forgive the voice for trying to protect me from what it didn't understand. Then, I had to apply that thought process into more areas of my life, parents, siblings, family, friends, strangers, and most of all, myself.

You must find the place
inside yourself
where nothing is
impossible.

Deepak K. Chopra

Action exercises

Write out the answers to the questions below. Even better, also discuss the questions and your answers with a loved one.

1. Who do you need to forgive?

   _____

   _____

   _____

   _____

2. Why haven't you forgiven them?

   _____

   _____

   _____

   _____

3. Where have you made mistakes in your own life?

   _____

   _____

_____

_____

4. Do you need to forgive yourself?

_____

_____

_____

_____

5. Is it hard for you to forgive yourself? If so, why?

_____

_____

_____

_____

6. What would it feel like to genuinely for-give yourself?

_____

_____

_____

---

*It's during
our darkest
moments
that we must
focus
to see the light.*

Aristotle

Chapter 10

If it's worth having, it's hard to get.

Throughout my life, people have accused me of being stubborn. If you ask my family, they would probably refer to me as a brat. Not because I got what I wanted, but because once I came to a decision, I wouldn't budge.

I suppose that is why, at the time, leaving college bothered me as much as it did. I was fixated on that goal and didn't accomplish it. Leaving college was the first big diversion from a goal. Education was critical. Both my parents and two of my elder siblings had degrees. I felt that I had given up on my goal and allowed the voice in my head to torture me for years.

My fundamental goal had not changed. I

wanted to make the world a better place. By leaving engineering, I didn't give up on the goal; I simply adjusted the path I would take. Along the way, I picked up additional skills to help me accomplish my fundamental goal.

Another aspect of perceived personal failure was with my inability to keep friends. I am the daughter of a military man, and I married a military man. All my life, I have moved about every three years. The constant moving made it difficult to stay connected, especially before the internet and social media. I often mourned leaving friends every time we moved. What made it worse was that I failed at staying in contact with them.

I prefer a small close network of friendships. Some people would do anything for popularity. Sometimes, to have many friends, you have to lose yourself. Unfortunately, many of those friends gained are friends in name only. Popularity is fleeting. In today's reality show culture, it seems people will do anything for attention and they don't care if it is good or bad - a few celebrities come to mind. It's harder to find true friends but, in the end, it is much more rewarding. I found that when my family moved to a new area, it was easier to keep my distance from most people. That method worked well, and I had many casual friends, but there are few that have known me well since my youth in the Philippines. Friends come and go, but the best friends stay.

Marriage was an area of life that I felt, early on, I would fail at. My parents had a rocky marriage that ended in divorce when I was seventeen. I thought, if that was what marriage was, I didn't want it. Additionally, I thought because I came from a broken home, I would not be able to have a healthy marriage. The voice was warning me to avoid getting married.

Throughout the early years of my mar-riage, I expected our relationship to sour. After about thirteen years of marriage, I was sure my good luck had run its course. I uncon-sciously began to sabotage our marriage. I'd stop talking for hours or go out with my girl-friends and not return home until the early hours of the following day. Our children were self-sufficient, and I felt useless. I believed my husband only appeared to love me because he "had" to. The voice in my head made sure every perceived slight offended me. The thought of failing and not being "good enough" infuriated me.

My stubborn streak returned, and I would demand my husband make my life with him better, or I would leave. Since I did not want to fail, I tried to push my husband away. I convinced myself that I was doing what he wanted. If he left, it would be his fault, not mine. I even tried to bribe him by saying I would let him take the children. I convinced myself that he cared for them more than he loved me.

I remember cornering him one day and asking directly, "Do you really love me or do you just need a maid and a babysitter?" and "I know you'd rather be with someone else; why are you wasting time with me?"

Michael was taken aback. He had no idea where these thoughts were coming from or what he had done wrong. He asked that we sit down and discuss what I was feeling. Sure enough, together we discovered that I was bored with my life and wanted to give up on our marriage so I could seek what would help me feel whole again. We learned that I felt as if my mind was withering away. I needed something to keep me mentally challenged.

My husband is a smart man who was far more grounded and committed to saving our marriage than I believed I could ever be. I had tried for years to finish my bachelor's degree, but every time we moved, I felt as if I had to start over to acquire enough credits from my new school to graduate. Finally, I was able to transfer all my divergent credits back to a sister school to my original college and received my degree! But I wasn't done chasing the paper to prove I had a brain.

My husband quickly realized that I

needed a challenge to feel worthy. He suggested I continue my education since I love to learn. I found an accelerated master's degree program to occupy my brain. Once my mind was preoccupied, the voice in my head stopped telling me how useless I was.

I finished my master's degree program in one year. That education opened doors to jobs I had no idea existed. Judging our relationship through the perception of my mental state became less frequent. I stopped analyzing Michael's intentions. He took assignments where I could be near my family and friends. A few short years later, Michael retired from the United States Air Force and accepted a job as a military contractor. After 20 years of me supporting him, we decided it was now time for him to support me with my career. It was a conscious decision to support the health of our family unit over his military career.

Michael and I reflect back to that time in our marriage where I was ready to walk away because I misunderstood my need to grow as an individual as a failure of our marriage. Marriage takes friendship, love, communication and a commitment to rekindle the connectedness that brought you together. If it's worth having, it's hard to get.

People are like water. When their path becomes blocked, they either become stagnant or build up energy/potential to burst through the blockage or find another way. Remember, the goal is more important than the path. Avoid becoming stuck in a rut. Keep pushing forward. Don't give up on you.

Be stubborn
about your goals,
and flexible
about
your methods.

Unknown

Action exercises

Write out the answers to the questions below. Even better, also discuss the questions and your answers with a loved one.

1. What is the difference between being stubborn and being committed?

   _____

   _____

   _____

   _____

2. When you give up on something, how do you explain it to yourself?

   _____

   _____

   _____

   _____

3. Do you identify good reasons why you are stopping?

_____

_____

_____

_____

4. What is the upside of giving up in these areas?

_____

_____

_____

_____

5. What is the downside of giving up in these areas?

_____

_____

_____

_____

6. What reasons for stopping have you not considered?

_____

_____

_____

_____

_____

*Only I
can change
my life.
No one
can do it
for me.*

_____

Carol Burnett

Chapter 11

Where is my "Why"?

Do you have someone who you look up to? I have many, but there are three that especially contribute to my positive mentality.

CONVICTION: Dr. Martin Luther King, Jr. has always fascinated me. When I was a young teen, I watched a video of him giving his 'I Have A Dream' speech; I felt chills run down my spine. I wanted to hold a strong conviction for whatever I did in life as he did for equality.

CONFIDENCE: Muhammad Ali, the world-renowned heavyweight champion boxer was a powerful force of nature. His stage presence and confidence were contagious! I remember watching him in the ring with George Foreman, who was larger and domineering, yet my family still cheered wildly for Ali. I want the confidence he had for whatever I am doing.

PASSION: I had the good fortune of hearing Maya Angelou recite a poem. I longed to weave emotion into words as she did. She made her words seem effortless as if they flowed through her heart and soul. I want to communicate with passion and emotion.

Each of these role models exhibit completely different strengths. I wonder, "How do they know what to do?" When people asked me what I wanted to be when I grew up, I would answer "Happy." Having the qualities of those people I admired would make me happy.

None of my role models were perfect. Each had to work hard and develop their gifts. Nothing came easy for them. Each made positive changes in the world in completely different ways. I've learned that discovering one's purpose is an important part of the "why" you are gifted in particular areas. Have you ever questioned "why" you are exceptionally talented in one or many areas? Have you pursued honing one or all those gifts?

Did you just say to yourself, "I'm not exceptional at anything?" If you did, let's reframe that statement. Take the voice in your head out of the equation and frame it positively. For example, "I'm exceptionally fantastic at being me." Do you really believe you are exceptionally gifted at nothing? Why do you believe that? Is it a result of residual words you heard as a child? What fuels this thought?

Here's something I learned the hard way that I'd like you to ponder.

Do you believe in a higher power?

If so, do you believe this being is perfect, magnificent and beautiful?

Are we not created in the image of this higher being? Would this being create a flawed design?

If you believe any of the above is true, how can you possibly believe you are not phenomenal?

If you don't believe in anything but pure chaos theory, even the randomness of everything that developed on this earth is still geometrically perfect, magnificent and beautiful. Correct?

Your simple existence is cosmically amazing. So, how can you think you are a flaw?

---

*Be careful how
you are talking
to yourself,
because
you are listening.*

Lisa M. Hayes

I believe that we are all designed with a special combination of gifts that no one else possesses. It is our life's purpose to discover what those gifts are and develop them to be the best version of ourselves.

It's been my experience that we actually know our gifts and that we deny ourselves pursuing the development of these gifts out of fear of the unknown. The voice in our head that tells us, "You aren't good enough," "What makes you think you're so special", "You aren't meant to be happy," and so on, keeps us paralyzed with fear. Over time we often come close to breaking free, and then something occurs that scares us back from developing our gifts.

Here's a secret... when you have a desire to accomplish something and there is a task between you and your desire that terrifies and prevents you from pursuing that desire... that task is exactly what you need to do. This fearful task, once accomplished, will give you the confidence to overcome any other challenge in your life.

Here is a test
to determine
if your life's
goal is complete.
If you are alive, it isn't.

Richard Bach

Action exercises

Write out the answers to the questions below. Even better, also discuss the questions and your answers with a loved one.

1. Do you know why you are here?

   _____

   _____

   _____

   _____

2. What do you do well? Would you consider it your gift?

   _____

   _____

   _____

   _____

3. Do you know anyone who passionately pursues their purpose?

   _____

_____

_____

_____

4. What difference does it make in their life?

_____

_____

_____

_____

5. If you don't know your purpose, are you spending some time everyday looking for it?

_____

_____

_____

_____

---

*Life has
no limitations,
except the
ones you make.*

Les Brown

Chapter 12

Summary

If you think you are
beaten, you are.

If you think you dare not, you
don't.

If you like to win, but think
you can't,

it's almost certain

you won't.

If you think you'll lose, you're
lost.

For out in the world we find,
success begins

with a fellow's will - It's all in
the state of mind.

If you think you're

outclassed, you are.

You have to think high to rise,
you've got

to be sure of yourself
before you can ever
win a prize.
Life's battles don't
always go to the stronger or
the faster man,
but sooner or later the man
who wins is the man who
thinks he can.

Napoleon Hill

We've finished the first round of questions relating to your goal (or refined goal). Now, look back at your goal as well as the answers to the questions.

How do you feel?

Reflect back to how you felt about yourself and your ability to reach a goal at the start of this book. How has your perspective changed?

Use the questions in this book for every goal

you wish to conquer. Additional questions may pop into your mind as you go through each chapter - write them down! Trust your instincts. The voice in your head is simply there to keep you safe based on the experiences it has from your past and from what you've witnessed throughout it all.

Imagine the voice in your head as a guardian who is searching a giant database of everything that has ever happened around or to you. The stories I have shared with you are intended to help your mind associate a situation in your memory with how I addressed situations simply to provide your brain and your protective voice in your head with possibilities.

Basically, the stories are adding to your mental database. Once you can rationalize with the voice in your head that there is a way around your perceived issue, the voice will step aside. The questions that I ask in this book are high-level on purpose. They force your mind to develop a course of action for your particular situation and help you see what is best for your success.

You are a magnificent human. You can accomplish anything you set your mind to. Granted, you can't spontaneously sprout wings and fly, but you can and will reach heights the former thinking version of you would have never thought possible. You will walk hand in hand with the voice in your head enjoying a relationship that is mutually respectful.

---

*Change is an
emotional journey.
It's not rainbows
and butterflies
through a field of daisies.
Change is uncomfortable
and forces you
to evaluate who you are.
The beauty is in the
possibilities.*

Michelle Mras

Closing thoughts...

T hank you for sharing your journey with me. Remember you can flip through and re-address the questions whenever you are faced with a choice and your inner voice becomes over protective.

Everyone has an inner voice of doubt. It takes effort to overcome that voice, our inner critic. People that you see succeeding where you wish to succeed are compromising and conquering the negative voice. You can do the same.

Your mind now has building blocks of examples from my past and your past to understand that you are capable and don't need to be protected as strongly as you have been.

I've been told, "You are so lucky!" throughout my life. I assure you, luck has nothing to do with it. Perseverance, lots of introspection, asking myself the hard questions on why I behave the way I do, being prepared for possibilities and being willing to try, are big players in "luck".

My definition of "LUCK":

When opportunity collides with effort:

It's not luck.
You create your
own opportunities.
Your potential is already in you.
The secret is in overcoming you.

Michelle Mras

---

*You are braver than
you believe,*

*STRONGER than
you seem,*

*and smarter than
you think.*

A.A. Milne

NOTES

NOTES

NOTES

NOTES

NOTES

_____

_____

_____

_____

_____

_____

_____

_____

_____

_____

_____

_____

_____

_____

_____

_____

_____

_____

_____

_____

_____

_____

_____

_____

_____

NOTES

NOTES

NOTES

_____

_____

_____

_____

_____

_____

_____

_____

_____

_____

_____

_____

_____

_____

_____

_____

_____

_____

_____

_____

_____

_____

NOTES

NOTES

NOTES

_____
_____
_____
_____
_____
_____
_____
_____
_____
_____
_____
_____
_____
_____
_____
_____
_____
_____
_____
_____
_____
_____
_____
_____

NOTES

NOTES

_____

_____

_____

_____

_____

_____

_____

_____

_____

_____

_____

_____

_____

_____

_____

_____

_____

_____

_____

_____

_____

_____

_____

_____

NOTES

NOTES

_____

_____

_____

_____

_____

_____

_____

_____

_____

_____

_____

_____

_____

_____

_____

_____

_____

_____

_____

_____

_____

_____

_____

_____

_____

NOTES

NOTES

_____

_____

_____

_____

_____

_____

_____

_____

_____

_____

_____

_____

_____

_____

_____

_____

_____

_____

_____

_____

_____

_____

_____

NOTES

NOTES

NOTES